REFLECTIONS

Copyright © 2019 Billy Carr Sr.

All rights reserved. This book or any portion thereof may not be reproduced or used in any manner whatsoever without the express written permission of the publisher except for the use of brief quotations in a book review.

Printed in the United States of America

First Printing, 2019

ISBN: 978-1-7333327-1-2   (Kindle)
ISBN: 978-1-7333327-2-9   (Paperback)

www.BG2G.us
www.BG2G.Shop

BG2G® DISCLAIMER OF AUTONOMY

BG2G is a Religious Corporation. Members and guests of BG2G sponsored events are 100% autonomous in their views, thoughts, behaviors and opinions expressed; and as a result topics may offend. By engaging with BG2G products and services you agree that all persons are individually responsible for their own behavior and speech at all times.

BG2G is a Federally Registered Service Trademark.

All Rights Reserved.

REFLECTIONS

POEMS OF FAITH

Pastor Billy Carr Sr.

TABLE OF CONTENTS

INTRODUCTION: WE MUST WALK ON 7
ACKNOWLEDGMENT 9
A WARM HEART 10
ALWAYS A FRIEND 12
ANOTHER CHANCE 14
APPLE PIE 15
AWESOME GOD 17
BABIES AND BILLS 19
BIG MAN 21
BLACK GIRL 22
BLACK MAN 23
BROTHERS 25
CONSEQUENCES 26
DADDY'S BABY GIRL 28
DEDICATED TO A NURSE 30
DIAMOND IN THE ROUGH 31
DISCIPLINE 33
EVERYDAY BLESSINGS 35
FAMILY 36
FOR OUR SISTERS 38
FUNNY MAN 39
GENERATION X 40
GLAMOUR GIRL 42

GOD IS GOOD	43
GOD'S DAUGHTERS	45
GOD'S FRIEND	46
GOD'S MIGHTY WARRIORS	47
GOD'S TREASURE CHEST	48
GOD'S WAY	50
GRANDMA	52
HEALED	53
I BELIEVE	54
I CRY	56
I LOVE YOU JESUS	57
IMAGES	59
IT YET APPEARS	60
L I F E	61
LEAD ME LORD	63
LET IT GO	65
LIFE IS FULL OF MYSTERY	66
LITTLE CHILDREN PRAISE	67
LITTLE JR.	68
LOVE WON	69
ME, YOU AND ALI BOO	71
MY FAVORITE PLACE	72
MY FRIEND – JESUS ARMS	73
MY FRIEND	74
MY STORY	75

NO LONGER THERE	76
NOT BEING FREE	77
OBSTACLES	79
POVERTY AND PAIN	80
PUT IT DOWN	81
RADIANCE	82
SILENCE	83
SOMETIMES	84
SUCCESS – HOLD JESUS CLOSE	85
SUCCESS – ON THE ROAD	86
SUGAR PLUM	88
SUNNY DAYS	89
SWEETNESS	90
THANK YOU JESUS	91
THANKFUL	92
THAT SPECIAL THING	93
THE CHANNELS OF MY MIND	95
THE CHILDREN	97
THE COUNTRY PREACHER	98
THE DOCTOR	100
THE EFFECTS OF ABUSE	101
THE FLAWS	103
THE LADY	104
THE LIONESS	105
THE LITTLE CHILD	106

THE MASTER	107
THE NICKEL	108
THE OTHER SIDE OF LOVE	109
THE PARK	111
THE QUEEN	112
THE RAIN 2	113
THE SPARKLE	114
THE TEST OF LOVE	115
THE VIEW	116
VIOLENCE	118
WANDA	119
WE WHO WORE	121
WHEN LEAST EXPECTED	122
YOU WERE THERE	124

INTRODUCTION: WE MUST WALK ON

THE STORM WILL COME BUT WE MUST WALK ON, AS WE CONTINUE OUR JOURNEY WE CAN NOW SEE CLEAR.

THE FOG HAS LEFT, WE CAN SEE OURSELVES AS NEVER BEFORE.

WE HAVE PASSED THE TEST WE CAN NOW CONTINUE TO TRUST GOD.

OUR GOD WILL NEVER LEAVE US OR FORSAKE US IN OUR TIME OF NEED.

THERE WILL BE A TIME TO REPENT, A TIME TO HUMBLE OURSELVES, A TIME TO FORGIVE AND BE FORGIVEN.

IT WILL BE A TIME OF REFLECTION, AND NEW DIRECTION.

WE MUST CONTINUE TO PRAY FERVENTLY, THE STORM HAS COME TO BRING OUT OUR BEST.

WE MUST WALK ON LEAVING OLD THINGS BEHIND, WHILE WE CONTINUE TO TRUST GOD.

IT WILL GET BETTER, WE WILL RECOVER AND GOD WILL RESTORE.

WE MUST WALK ON, WE MUST WALK ON. WE HAVE ONLY COMPLETED PART OF OUR JOURNEY.

ACKNOWLEDGMENT

I WOULD LIKE TO THANK SO MANY. THIS BOOK COULD NOT HAVE COME TO PRINT WITHOUT THE HELP OF SO MANY OTHERS, YOU WERE THERE IN THE PLACE GOD HAD CHOSEN YOU TO BE AT THAT SEASON OF MY LIFE.

A WARM HEART

YOU WERE THERE FROM THE START, LOVE FLOWS FROM A WARM HEART.

YOU TOOK THE TIME TO PRAY FOR ME, YOU SAW THE THINGS I DID NOT SEE.

YOU SHOWED ME THE LOVE OF GOD, WHEN LIFE FOR ME WAS ROUGH AND HARD.

YOU TOOK ME TO BE YOUR FRIEND, WHEN ALL I HAD WAS A TOOTHLESS GRIN.

LOVE FLOWS FROM A WARM HEART,

FRIENDS FOREVER WE WILL STAND, WHEN WE HOLD ON TO JESUS HAND.

YOU CALL WHEN I NEED IT THE MOST, THE YEARS HAVE PASSED, WE HAVE BEEN SO CLOSE.

THERE WERE TIMES WHEN WE COULD NOT SEE, GOD'S AWESOME PLAN FOR YOU AND ME.

YOU WERE THERE FROM THE VERY START, LOVE FLOWS FROM A WARM HEART.

ALWAYS A FRIEND

A SOPHISTICATED LADY, SO SWEET AND NICE, SHE WAS MARRIED ONCE, BUT SHE SAYS NEVER TWICE,

WHAT ABOUT ALL THE THINGS HE PUT HER THROUGH, SHE CAN NOT GO THERE AGAIN NOT EVEN FOR YOU.

WILL YOU HANDLE HER WITH CARE, WHEN SHE CALLS WILL YOU BE THERE.

BE SLOW TRY NOT TO MOVE TOO FAST, HANDLE HER GENTLY SO FRIENDSHIP WILL LAST.

SHE TAKES WALKS IN THE PARK ON A WARM AFTERNOON, SHE LIKES GAZING AT THE STARS, THE LAMP POST, AND MOON.

SHE WAS LIVING HER LIFE LIKE SHE WANTED TO, SHE LOOKED AROUND AND THEN CAME YOU.

KNOCK AT HER DOOR BUT NEVER ENTER IN, SHE IS ALWAYS A LADY, ALWAYS A FRIEND.

ANOTHER CHANCE

THANK YOU LORD FOR ANOTHER CHANCE, THE DEVIL AND I NO LONGER DANCE.

IT MATTERS NOT HOW LIFE HAS BEEN, YOU GAVE ME ANOTHER CHANCE TO WIN.

WHEN I WAS LOW YOU COMFORTED ME, I AM NOW CLOSER THAN I USE TO BE,

WHAT A LOVING GOD SO AWESOME AND TRUE, SAID I WILL DO THIS JUST FOR YOU.

I AM NO LONGER ON THE GROUND, THE CHANGE YOU BROUGHT TURNED ME AROUND.

THE DEVIL AND I NO LONGER DANCE, THANK YOU LORD FOR ANOTHER CHANCE.

APPLE PIE

WE SING, WE DANCE, WE MISS THE ROMANCE, WITH GOD WE GET THE SECOND CHANCE.

I MAKE MY MONEY JUST LIKE YOU, THE THINGS WE SAY THE THINGS WE DO.

I GLANCE AT THE PICTURE AND WHAT DO I SEE, EQUAL OPPORTUNITY FOR YOU AND ME

WE LIVE OUR LIVES AND THEN WE DIE, JUST GIVE ME A PIECE OF THIS APPLE PIE.

THE DOORS ARE OPEN SO STEP RIGHT IN, THERE ARE SO MANY FENCES WE HAVE TO MEND.

THE LOVE OF GOD WILL SEE US THROUGH, IT WILL TAKE ME AND OH YES YOU.

BRING ALONG LOVE AND COMPASSION TOO. ONE THING I

DESIRE BEFORE I DIE, JUST GIVE ME A PIECE OF THIS APPLE PIE.

AWESOME GOD

HE RULES SUPREME OVER ALL, HE HOLDS US UP LEST WE FALL.

HE IS THE OBJECT OF LIFE'S STORY, HE IS COMING AGAIN IN ALL HIS GLORY.

GOD SENT HIS SON IN FLESH LIKE MAN, HE IS THE ONLY TRUE GOD, UNDERSTAND.

OUR AWESOME GOD, OUR AWESOME GOD.

HE TAKES US IN FROM THE STREET, WE SHOULD LIVE FOREVER AT JESUS FEET.

GOD CREATED THE MOON AND THE STARS. TROUT, BASS, JUPITER, AND MARS.

HE SENDS THE LIGHTING AND THE RAIN, WE WALK AWAY COME BACK AGAIN.

OUR AWESOME GOD, OUR AWESOME GOD.

BABIES AND BILLS

I PRAY FOR YOUNG MOTHERS AS THEY CLIMB THE HILLS, I SEE THEM WITH BABIES AND I KNOW THEY HAVE BILLS.

LORD HELP THEM TO SEE THAT YOU ARE THERE, IN THE GOOD AND BAD TIMES AND THAT YOU ALWAYS CARE.

HELP THEM TO PRAY AND LEAVE THINGS IN YOUR HANDS, ALTHOUGH THE STORMS OF LIFE BLOWS, THEY KNOW YOU STILL CAN.

PLEASE SHOW THEM THE WAY AS THEY LOOK UNTO YOU; OPEN THEIR EYES LET THEM SEE SOMETHING NEW.

MOST OF ALL TOUCH THEIR HEARTS AND FILL IT WITH LOVE, AND NO MATTER THE CLIMB THEY CAN LOOK UP ABOVE.

I PRAY FOR THE MOTHERS AS THEY CLIMB THE HILLS, LORD YOU GAVE

THEM THE BABIES AND THOSE ARE YOUR BILLS.

BIG MAN

HE TOOK THE TIME TO SAY HELLO, I WOULD SEE HIM GOING TO AND FRO.

HE WAS A MAN OF FAITH, A MAN WITH LOVE, A MAN THAT WAS GENTLE AS A DOVE.

HE WALKED WITH HIS BIBLE IN HIS HAND, THE MAN OF FAITH I CALLED BIG MAN.

HE LOOKED LIKED HE HAS BEEN THROUGH THE WAR, HIS FACE STILL HAD THE BATTLE SCAR.

AS HE WOULD MAKE IT THROUGH THE DAY, HE WOULD STOP BY THE CHURCH, TAKE TIME TO PRAY.

WHO WILL DO GOD'S WILL HE CASHED THE CHECK AND PAID THE BILL.

BIG MAN LEFT US A FEW WEEKS AGO, THANK GOD WE ARE STILL HERE, TO SAY HELLO.

BLACK GIRL

BEAUTIFUL BLACK GIRL WITH YOUR SMILE, LOOKING LIKE THE QUEEN OF THE NILE.

SUCH BEAUTIFUL SKIN NOT A HAIR OUT OF PLACE, I STARE AS I LOOK AT YOUR DARK BROWN FACE.

JUST ONE MORE GLANCE AS I WALK OUT OF THE DOOR, I MAY NEVER SEE YOUR LOVELY FACE ANYMORE.

SOME PEOPLE SIT UP STRAIGHT, OTHERS HAVE A LEAN, YOU HAVE THE POSE OF AN AFRICAN QUEEN.

BLACK MAN

YOU ONCE WALKED AS KINGS OF THE EARTH, YOU WITNESS THE ANNOUNCEMENT OF JESUS BIRTH.

THE MAN THAT ONCE WAS VERY WISE, NOW THEY WANT US TO BELIEVE THE LIES.

YOUR QUEEN WAS CLOSEST TO YOUR HEART, SHE WAS VERY BEAUTIFUL AND VERY SMART.

YOUR CHILDREN WORE THE BEST THAT MONEY COULD BUY, GOD CALLED THEM THE APPLE OF HIS EYE.

BLACK MAN, BLACK MAN, DON'T WALK AWAY, THE WORLD NEED MEN LIKE YOU TODAY.

THE KIDS SAY WHERE IS DADDY, WHERE DID HE GO,

HE DID NOT COME BY TO PLAY WITH US OR TAKE US TO THE STORE.

THE WORLD OUT THERE WILL FOOL US AS WE CHASE OUR HOPES AND DREAMS,

WHEN WE WAKE UP WE WILL REALIZE LIFE IS SELDOM AS IT SEEMS.

WHEN WE HAVE TRAVELED THE ROAD, AND HAVE STOPPED TO REST AWHILE,

WE WILL FIND OUR ANSWER IN JESUS, NOT THE MONEY OR THE STYLE.

BROTHERS

THERE IS NO RACIAL DIVIDE, NO SECRETS TO HIDE WE ARE BROTHERS.

WE LOVE ONE ANOTHER, WE PROTECT ONE ANOTHER

NO HILL IS TOO HIGH OR VALLEY TOO LOW, WE WILL STAND AND FIGHT THE FOE.

WE ARE STRONG LIKE IRON, MOVE LIKE THE WIND, IF DEFEATED, WE RETURN AGAIN. WE ARE BROTHERS

WE TAKE THE RISK AND PAY THE PRICE, MOVE INTO ACTION AND DO NOT THINK TWICE.

WE TRAVEL THE GLOBE OVER AGAIN, WE ARE U S FIGHTING WOMEN AND MEN.

WE ARE BROTHERS

CONSEQUENCES

IN THE MIST OF THESE LAST DAYS; GOD IS SPEAKING IN SOME AWESOME WAYS.

HE IS CALLING HIS CHILDREN HE LOVES SO DEAR, GOD IS SPEAKING IN LOVE, WHY DON'T WE HEAR.

WE ACCEPT THINGS THAT SHOULD NOT BE, AS THE THINGS GOD APPROVES OF.

YET HE GIVES US GRACE AND MERCY BECAUSE OF HIS STEAD FAST LOVE.

HAVE WE LOST OUR ZEAL FOR GOD LOOKING THROUGH THE EYES OF WORLD,

WHEN WE SHOULD SEE THROUGH THE EYES OF JESUS.

THERE WILL BE CONSEQUENCES AND WE WILL NOT GET AWAY.

DO WE ALLOW THE HOLY SPIRIT TO GUIDE US IN A FALLEN WORLD

GET AWAY WITH WHAT YOU SAY INNOCENT LIVES TAKEN TOO SOON

CONFUSED CHILDREN GOING TO AND FRO, WHO IS DADDY, WHO IS MOMMY THEY DON'T KNOW.

WE ARE LIVING IN A FALLEN WORLD, IS THAT A BOY OR IS IT A GIRL

JAILS AND PRISONS FILLING FAST, PEOPLE WILL NOT LET GO THE PAST.

LORD I LIFT MY HANDS TO YOU, FOR ALL I KNOW THAT YOU WILL DO,

WE MUST FACE THE CONSEQUENCES.

DADDY'S BABY GIRL

MOTHERS LITTLE MUFFIN, DADDY'S BABY GIRL, WENT OUT TO PLAY ONE DAY, SHE GOT CAUGHT OUT IN THE WORLD.

CAN YOU FELL THE HURT AS SHE DEALS WITH HER PAIN, SHE HAS BEEN OUT IN THE COLD; SHE HAS BEEN SOAKED IN THE RAIN.

WHAT WILL PEOPLE SAY WHEN THEY SEE HER SHAME, SHE IS OUT THERE IN THE STREETS WILL IT EVER BE THE SAME.

SHE IS LIVING THE KIND OF LIFE THAT ALSO NEEDS A CHANGE, IT IS ONLY THROUGH JESUS THIS LIFE CAN BE ARRANGED.

BABY GIRL CAME TO THE ALTER AT THE ALTER CALL, SHE SAID PLEASE HELP ME JESUS I WILL GIVE YOU MY ALL.

MOTHERS SWEET LITTLE MUFFIN, DADDY'S BABY GIRL, GAVE HER LIFE

TO JESUS AND CAME OUT OF THE WORLD.

DEDICATED TO A NURSE

YEARS HAVE PASSED SINCE WE MET, A LADY LIKE YOU IS HARD TO FORGET.

DO THE POEMS OF LIFE REALLY RHYME, THINGS SO EASILY SLIP AWAY WITH TIME.

YOU WERE SO YOUNG, SO SWEET, SO SMART, YOU COULD QUICKLY STEAL A YOUNG MAN'S HEART.

I SEE ONE AND THINK OF TWO, WHAT IF I WRITE THIS POEM FOR YOU?

YOUR PRETTY BLACK HAIR BEAUTIFUL GRAY STREAK, YOU WAS ALWAYS A LADY, SO KIND AND MEEK.

YOU FELT THE THINGS I COULD NOT FEEL, WHEN THE LIFE I LIVED WAS OUT IN LEFT FIELD.

MAY GOD BLESS YOU FOR ALL YOU DO, THIS POEM I WRITE IS JUST FOR YOU.

DIAMOND IN THE ROUGH

I CAME TO JESUS LOOKING, HARD, MEAN AND TOUGH, BUT IN THE PLAN OF GOD I WAS A DIAMOND IN THE ROUGH.

JESUS YOU SAVED ME FROM A WORLD OF SIN, I KNOW IN YOU I WILL ALWAYS HAVE A FRIEND.

I NEVER GET CAUGHT UP IN THE THINGS PEOPLE DO, YOU ARE THE ONE THAT WILL ALWAYS BRING ME THROUGH.

I AM NOT CUT AND POLISHED, SO THE WORLD CAN NOT SEE, THE PRECIOUS JEWEL GOD IS MAKING ME.

ONE DAY JESUS WE KNOW IF WE HOLD TRUE, WE WILL BEAR THE LIKENESS OF YOU.

KINDNESS GENTLENESS LOVE AND FAITH, I STAND HERE TODAY BECAUSE OF YOUR GRACE.

I WAS THE MAN LOOKING HARD, MEAN, AND TOUGH, LORD YOU DID NOT LET ME STAY A DIAMOND IN THE ROUGH.

DISCIPLINE

WHEN THE WORD DISCIPLINE COMES TO MIND, I THINK OF YOU, WHEN I HEAR THE WORD LOVE, I THINK OF YOU.

WE HAVE NOT ONLY PASSED THE TEST, FOR YOU DEMANDED OUR VERY BEST.

YOU WERE FIRM, SMART AND STRONG, YOU SHOWED US LOVE, YOU TOOK US ON.

YOU KNEW WHAT ONE DAY WE COULD BE, WHEN OUR YOUNG BRIGHT EYES JUST COULD NOT SEE.

THE WORD CHARACTER, I THINK OF YOU, YOU TAUGHT US WHAT WAS RIGHT AND TRUE.

YOU WERE THE ONE THAT HELPED US PASS THE TEST, THE ONE THAT GAVE YOUR VERY BEST.

I WILL ALWAYS THINK OF YOU, WHENEVER I HEAR THE WORD DISCIPLINE.

EVERYDAY BLESSINGS

WHEN I AWAKE AND SEE THE SUN, I COUNT MY BLESSINGS MORE THAN ONE.

GOD IS SO GOOD WE STAND IN AWE, HIS WONDERFUL WORKS WE THANK HIM FOR ALL.

BLESSINGS SENT IN SO MANY WAYS, I WILL LIFT MY VOICE AND GIVE HIM PRAISE.

RECEIVE HIS BLESSINGS ONE BY ONE, IT IS SO GOOD TO KNOW HIS SON.

FAMILY

I PRAYED LORD AND YOU ANSWERED PRAYER, YOU SPOKE TO ME SAID I NEEDED TO BE THERE.

THE THINGS I HAVE DONE WAS NOT ALWAYS RIGHT, AND WE HAD THOSE DISCUSSIONS IN THE MIDDLE OF THE NIGHT.

THE TIMES I CRIED WHILE TEARS RAN DOWN MY FACE, YOU CAME AND GAVE ME COMFORT IN THAT VERY PLACE.

THERE WERE TIMES THAT MY WORLD SEEM TO TURN UPSIDE DOWN, YOUR GRACE AND YOUR MERCY TURNED EVERYTHING AROUND

LORD REGARDLESS OF WHAT LIFE HAS PUT ME THROUGH, ONE THING I KNOW FOR SURE IS THAT THE PRAISE BELONGS TO YOU.

THANK YOU FOR ANSWERED PRAYER, WE ARE TOGETHER AGAIN, WHEN I

COULD HAVE LOST IT ALL, LORD YOU STEPPED IN.

THINGS ARE NEVER ON OUR TIME, YET YOU ARE WORKING ALL THE WHILE,

I WILL LEAVE THINGS IN YOUR HANDS AND GO ON AND WALK THIS MILE.

FOR OUR SISTERS

WE HAVE WALKED AWAY FROM YOUR SIDE; SOME OF US FOR MONEY SOME OF US FOR PRIDE.

WE NEVER GAVE YOU THE LOVE AND RESPECT DUE, WHEN WE PROMISED A LOVE THAT WAS TRUE.

THE PAYMENT FOR OUR DEEDS ARE FAR BEHIND, WE TRY TO FORGET BUT THEY STILL COME TO MIND.

WHAT WOULD WE BE WITHOUT YOU ALL YOUR LOVE IS THERE WHEN WE SLIP AND FALL.

DO WE LOVE YOU LIKE WE ALWAYS SAY IS THE GAME OF LOVE PLAYED THE SAME WAY

GOOD DAYS AND BAD DAYS YOU ARE STILL THERE, TRYING TO SHOW US THAT YOU ALWAYS CARE.

TIME MOVES ALONG IN THIS LIFE WE LIVE, WE WOULD LIKE TO ASK WILL YOU PLEASE FORGIVE.

FUNNY MAN

THE CHILDREN CALL ME FUNNY MAN, I WAS OUT THERE WITH MY BUSINESS PLAN.

ICE CREAM ON ME, ICE CREAM ON ME, MEET ME AT THE TRUCK OVER BY THE TREE.

WE ARE GLAD TO SEE YOU FUNNY MAN, NOW TELL US SOMETHING NEW. WE HAD SO MUCH FUN THE LAST TIME, WHAT ARE YOU GOING TO DO

YOU SEE OUR SMILING FACES AS WE HAVE SO MUCH FUN, YOU SAY THAT WE ARE FUNNY BUT YOU ARE THE FUNNY ONE.

WE WILL SEE YOU LATER FUNNY MAN, RIGHT NOW WE HAVE TO RUN, WE THANK YOU FOR THE ICE CREAM; YES YOU ARE THE FUNNY ONE.

GENERATION X

CHILDREN THERE ARE THINGS YOU NEED TO KNOW, WHY DID WE FIGHT, SO YOU COULD GO.

RACISM AND SEGREGATION INTIMIDATION AND HUMILIATION, AND WE LIVE IN THE GREATEST NATION

YOU MUST KEEP GOING WITH HEADS HELD HIGH, AND GET YOUR PIECE OF THIS AMERICAN PIE.

THE WORK WAS HARD AND THE WAGES LOW, WE STOOD STRONG SO YOU COULD GO.

TAKE THIS THING ON OFF THE CHAIN, YOU HAVE NO REASON TO COMPLAIN.

GO ON AND AS YOU TAKE YOUR STAND, SHOW THE WORLD YOU ARE NOT THAT MAN,

THE MAN THEY SAY HAD THE MISGUIDED MIND, THE ONE THEY WANTED TO CONTROL OR CONFINE.

WE ONCE WAS LOCKED OUT SIDE THE GATE, WE HAD TO FIGHT WE HAD TO WAIT.

IT WAS ALL BECAUSE HE LOVED US SO, GOD WAS THERE SO YOU COULD GO.

GLAMOUR GIRL

THE LADY BEAMS WITH HER PRETTY SMILE, SHE SITS DOWN JUST TO REST AWHILE.

I WOULD NOT TRY ANYTHING FUNNY, THE LOVELY LADY WORKS HARD FOR HER MONEY.

SUCH A BEAUTIFUL FACE, LOOKING OUT OF PLACE. WHEN IT COMES TO STYLE SHE REALLY HAS TASTE.

SHE LOOKS AND SMILES WITH NOT MUCH TO SAY, DRESSED SO NICE, LOOKING STUNNING EVERYDAY.

SHE IS THIS BEAUTIFUL LADY, TRYING TO MAKE IT IN THE WORLD, WE ALL CALL HER GLAMOUR GIRL.

GOD IS GOOD

WE SEE THE FIELDS WHITE FULL OF SNOW; RUN OUT THE COLD AND SHUT THE DOOR.

WE SIT AND WATCH THE CHILDREN PLAY, WE WISH OUR NEIGHBORS A JOYFUL DAY

GOD PROVIDES THE THINGS WE NEED, FOR EVERY PLANT THERE IS A SEED.

HIS GOODNESS AND MERCY OVERFLOWS, THE EAGLE FLY'S AWAY IT GOES.

THE MOUNTAINS ARE FILLED WITH MORNING DEW, GOD FEEDS THE BIRDS HE CARES FOR YOU.

GOD IS GOOD, GOD IS GOOD.

THE YEARS WILL COME AND PASS AWAY, GOD'S WORD WILL STAND IT IS HERE TO STAY.

WE SEE HIS WONDERS, WE FEEL THE WIND, WE RECEIVE HIS SON AND ARE BORN AGAIN.

GOD'S DAUGHTERS

LOVING WOMEN GIFTED AND SMART, SOME TELL THE STORIES THAT WILL BREAK THE HEART.

A HELLO, GOOD MORNING, A GENTLE NOD, THESE ARE THE WOMEN WHO WALK WITH GOD.

STANDING FOR JESUS IS THE LIFE THEY LIVE, THEY HAVE SO MUCH TO LIVE FOR, SO MUCH TO GIVE.

THEY BEAR THE PAIN THEY WEAR THE SCAR, THE WORLD CANNOT SEE THE JEWELS THEY ARE.

SOME GET MISTREATED ALONG THE WAY, THEY WILL LEAVE THINGS TO JESUS FOR HE WILL REPAY.

GOD'S FRIEND

LEAD BY THE SPRIT, ACTING ON LOVE, LIVING THE LIFE AS FREE AS A DOVE.

FULL OF COMPASSION, DISTANT FROM SIN, REACHING OUT TO OTHERS AGAIN AND AGAIN.

TEACHING GOD'S PEOPLE, PREACHING HIS WORD, WE WILL TRY TO REMEMBER THE SERMONS WE HAVE HEARD.

MAY GOD EVER BLESS US AND SHOW US THE WAY, WE KNOW THAT JESUS WILL RETURN ONE DAY.

GOD'S FRIEND, MY FRIEND, THE LORD'S SERVANT.

GOD'S MIGHTY WARRIORS

WE ARE GOD'S MIGHTY WARRIORS, WE TRAVEL THE ROCKY ROAD.

GOD FIGHTS OUR BATTLES, GOD BEARS OUR HEAVY LOAD.

HE WILL PROVIDE THE THINGS WE NEED, HIS HOLY WORD WE SHOULD ALWAYS HEED.

HE LEADS US IN THE LIGHT OF HIS WORD, HE STRENGTHEN OUR HAND SETS US FREE AS A BIRD.

WE ARE GOD'S MIGHTY WARRIORS, WE HAVE SWORDS IN OUR HANDS,

WE PRAISE HIS HOLY NAME.

GOD'S TREASURE CHEST

FOR JUST ONE PEEK IN GOD'S TREASURE CHEST, WOULD YOU PICK UP YOUR SHOES AND PUT AWAY YOUR DRESS.

JUST FOR ONE STONE SHINING BRIGHT, WOULD YOU CLEAN YOUR ROOM AND PRAY TONIGHT.

WOULD YOU DO YOUR LESSONS AND FIX YOUR HAIR, COULD YOU TRY TO TREAT YOUR SISTER FAIR?

FOR JUST ONE PEEK, FOR JUST ONE PEEK.

WOULD YOU HELP THE OLD MAN DOWN THE STREET, COULD YOU BRING HIM SOMETHING GOOD TO EAT?

THE MASTER HAS ALL THINGS WAITING FOR YOU, SHINING COLORS, PURPLE, RED AND BLUE.

WOULD YOU BE GOOD TODAY, TRY TO WALK IN HIS WAY. FOR JUST ONE PEEK, FOR JUST ONE PEEK.

GOD'S WAY

LET THINGS ALONE THAT SHOULD NOT BE, GOD'S EVER WATCHING EYES WILL SEE.

GOD RULES THE NIGHT AND BRINGS THE DAY, WE SHOULD LET IT BE HIS WAY.

DURING GOOD TIMES AND TROUBLED DAYS, GOD WILL DO WHAT HIS WORD SAYS.

THE THINGS OF LIFE THAT WE GO THROUGH, GOD'S LOVE IS ALWAYS THERE FOR YOU.

HE TAKES AWAY HEARTACHE AND PAIN, SHELTERS US FROM COLD AND RAIN.

WHEN DISASTER COMES HE SENDS ALARM, HE WILL PROTECT US FROM ALL HARM.

SOMETIMES WE DO NOT KNOW WHAT TO DO, GOD HAS A PLAN THAT IS RIGHT FOR YOU.

WHEN TROUBLE SEEM TO COME TO MIND, GOD HAS A WAY THAT IS SWEET AND KIND.

GOD RULES THE NIGHT AND BRINGS THE DAY, LET IT ALWAYS BE GOD'S WAY.

GRANDMA

HONEY HE WILL NOT MARRY YOU, HE WILL DO AS YOU LET HIM DO.

SHE TOLD THE YOUNG GIRLS WHAT IT WAS ABOUT, I HAVE SEEN THEM STAND AND CURSE HER OUT.

STILL GRANDMA STOOD HER GROUND, STILL GRANDMA NEVER BACKED DOWN

DO NOT GO DOWN TO HIS HOUSE TONIGHT, I FEEL THERE IS GOING TO BE A FIGHT...

WHILE GRANDMA HAS LEFT AND GONE AWAY, THE WORDS SHE SPOKE ARE WITH ME TO STAY

STILL GRANDMA STOOD HER GROUND, STILL GRANDMA NEVER BACKED DOWN.

HEALED

HEALED BECAUSE YOU LOVE ME SO,
HEALED THE TEARS NO LONGER FLOW.

HEALED YOU SET MY SPIRIT FREE,
THE PEACE OF GOD SURPASSES ME.

HEALED THAT I CAN TRULY STAND,
AND WALK UPRIGHT AS A GODLY MAN.

I CAN LEAN ON YOU WHEN I AM NOT STRONG, YOU GIVE ME THE STRENGTH TO CARRY ON.

HEALED AS YOUR WITNESS LIVING AND TRUE; HEALED I CAN GIVE ALL THE PRAISE TO YOU.

I HAVE A BRAND NEW LIFE AND ANOTHER START,

HEALED I HAVE A VERY HUMBLE HEART.

I BELIEVE

THAT EVERYBODY IS SOMEBODY ONCE WE FIND OURSELVES,

THAT THE MIND CAN UNLOCK THE DOOR TO MANY MYSTERIES.

THAT INNER PEACE AND INNER STRENGTH GO HAND AND HAND,

THAT MANY THINGS GO INTO THE MAKING OF A MAN.

THAT HEAVEN CRIES WHEN IT RAINS,

THAT HEAVEN SMILES WHEN THE SUN SHINES.

I BELIEVE THAT FAITH, HOPE AND CHARITY ARE SISTERS, AND BROTHERS EACH DEPENDENT UPON THE OTHER.

I BELIEVE THAT GOD RULES SUPREME,

THAT LOVE MUST COME BEFORE THERE IS PEACE.

THESE ARE THE BELIEFS OF A MERE MAN, I WANT YOU TO TRY TO UNDERSTAND.

I AM NOT A GENIUS OR DEAN'S LIST GRAD,

I JUST WOKE UP ONE MORNING AND REALIZED,

THAT MY BELIEF IN GOD WAS ALL I REALLY HAD.

I CRY

TOMORROW YOU GO VIETNAM…I CRY,

MEMORIES OF THE PAST, ALONE AGAIN…I CRY.

SOLDIERS COME AND SOLDIERS GO, THEY DO NOT COME BACK ANY MORE.

I THINK I COULD HAVE BEEN HIS WIFE, HE LOVES AND LEAVES AND THAT'S HIS LIFE…I CRY.

WE WERE SO CLOSE I WILL MISS YOU SO, PLEASE DO NOT FORGET ME WHEN YOU GO.

I SIT AND DRINK MY CUP OF TEA, MAY GOD ONE DAY SEND YOU BACK TO ME.

TOMORROW YOU GO VIETNAM…I CRY,

DEEP DOWN IN MY HEART I DIE.

I LOVE YOU JESUS

YOU ARE THE ONE THAT CHANGED MY LIFE, I LOVE YOU MORE AND MORE.

I WILL FOREVER LIVE FOR YOU; I HAVE MUCH TO THANK YOU FOR.

THERE WERE THOSE TIMES YOU SPOKE TO ME, IN GOOD TIMES AND IN BAD, THOSE SPECIAL TIMES WE SHEARED, ARE THE BEST THAT I HAVE HAD.

I LOVE YOU JESUS AND PRAISE YOUR NAME, YOU GAVE ME A THANKFUL HEART, I HAVE NOT DONE ALL I SHOULD, BUT LORD YOU DID YOUR PART.

YOU DREW ME IN SO MANY WAYS, CLOSER I HAVE COME TO YOU, YOU TAUGHT ME SO MANY THINGS, IN THE STORMS YOU BROUGHT ME THROUGH.

I LOVE YOU JESUS AND GIVE YOU PRAISE, I WILL FOREVER MORE, I AM

OH SO GLAD I LET YOU IN, WHEN YOU KNOCKED AT MY DOOR.

IMAGES

JET PLANES SUDDENLY APPEAR,
THEY DO NOT KNOW DEATH IS NEAR.

HIGH UP IN THE SKIES TODAY, BOMBS ARE DROPPED AND THEY FLY AWAY.

BLOOP THERE IS THAT SOUND,

FIRE BALLS RISING HIGH, IMAGES OF DAYS GONE BY.

WHY DID IT HAVE TO BE? WHAT IF IT WERE YOU OR ME,

PEOPLE RUNNING, PEOPLE SCREAMING,

WAR WAS ROUGH BUT WHAT'S THE MEANING.

IMAGES, IMAGES, BLOOP,

FIRE BALLS RISING HIGH, NOW I SIT AND WONDER WHY.

IT YET APPEARS

I CAN STILL SEE YOUR FACE, AS I LOOK AT YOUR SON.

I CAN STILL HEAR YOUR VOICE, YOU WILL ALWAYS BE THE ONE.

WE WILL MISS YOU GOING ON, GOD GAVE YOU A BETTER HOME.

GOD HAD A BETTER PLAN, NOW HE HOLDS YOU IN HIS HAND.

WE WILL REMEMBER YOUR SMILE, WE MUST WALK THIS EARTHLY MILE.

WE WILL WIPE AWAY OUR TEARS, AS WE PASS THROUGH THE YEARS.

HE HAS GIVEN PEACE AND CALM, THROUGH THE THIRTY SECOND PSALM.

IT YET APPEARS THAT YOU ARE STILL HERE.

LIFE

WOULD GOD BE PLEASED WITH ME AND YOU? BY THE THINGS WE SAY AND WHAT WE DO.

THE LIFE WE LIVE SHOULD LIFT UP HIS NAME, AND WE CAN LIVE AND NOT HAVE THE SHAME.

WHEN WE SPEAK LOVE IS IT FOR REAL, TO HELP THE ONES WHO ARE WOUNDED STILL.

WILL WE TEACH THE LESSON TO BE HEARD? BY THE WAY IT IS LINED UP WITH GOD'S WORD.

WE SHOULD NOT WORRY WHAT OTHERS SAY, AS WE GIVE OURSELVES TO THE LORD AND PRAY.

THERE ARE VARIOUS THINGS WE WILL GO THROUGH, THE EXCEPTIONS ARE NOT FOR ME OR YOU.

THESE THINGS WILL COME BUT WILL NOT LAST LONG, THE VERY REASON

THEY COME IS TO MAKE THE WEAK STRONG.

LEAD ME LORD

I AM OUT HERE IN THE GRIPS OF SIN, THE PAIN IS WORST THAN IT HAS EVER BEEN.

LEAD ME BACK FORGIVE ME MORE, I HAVE DRIFTED AWAY FROM THE ONLY SHORE.

I AM NOT THE MAN THAT I SHOULD BE, WAS NOT FAMILY OR FRIENDS LORD, IT WAS ME.

AFTER THE LIFE I CHOSE TO LIVE, YOU ARE READY AND WILLING TO FORGIVE.

LEAD ME BACK LORD, I AM LOST, SHOW ME LORD THE WAY OF THE CROSS.

LEAD ME BACK SO I CAN BE, THE MAN OF GOD YOU DESIRE FOR ME.

LORD LEAD ME BACK SO I CAN DO, THE THINGS I KNOW YOU WANT ME TO.

SAVE ME, WASH ME, MAKE ME CLEAN,
LORD GENTLY LEAD ME HOME AGAIN.

LET IT GO

YOUNG MAN HOLDING THE RESULTS OF PAIN, GOD SAYS GIVE UP THE GAME, LET GO OF THE GUILT AND SHAME.

WHY DID YOU COMMIT THE CRIME?

I DO NOT KNOW

GIVE UP THE RAGE AND LET IT GO.

GOD HAS THE KEY TO UNLOCK YOUR MIND, ACCEPT HIS WORD GET BACK IN LINE.

WHY CHOOSE THE GUN,

I DO NOT KNOW

FALL ON YOUR KNEES AND LET IT GO.

LIFE IS FULL OF MYSTERY

LIFE IS FULL OF MYSTERY, THE WAY GOD DEALS WITH YOU AND ME.

WE THINK WE HAVE IT ALL WORKED OUT, WHILE SECOND THOUGHT THERE IS SOME DOUBT.

SOME THINGS ARE NOT FOR US TO SEE, WHILE GOD SAYS LEAVE IT ALL TO ME.

MANY TIMES WE FEEL WE JUST CAN'T COPE, THEN WHEN WE THINK WE HAVE LOST ALL HOPE,

GOD SAYS, PROBLEM SOLVED ERASES THE BLACKBOARD.

LITTLE CHILDREN PRAISE

LET THE CHILDREN PRAISE HIM, THEY ARE THE APPLES OF HIS EYE, THEY DANCE WITH ALL THEIR MIGHT, FLOAT LIKE A BUTTERFLY.

MY HEART IS TOUCHED IN THESE LAST DAYS, WHEN THE CHILDREN ARISE AND GIVE GOD PRAISE.

THEY DANCE; THEY DANCE WITH ALL THEIR MIGHT, OH LORD IT IS SUCH A BEAUTIFUL SIGHT.

SOMETIMES THEY DANCE OTHER TIMES THEY SING, LIKE THE SOUND OF AN ANGLE MOVING HIS WINGS.

THE CHILDREN LOVE JESUS AND THIS IS TRUE, HE HAS ALWAYS BEEN THERE FOR ME AND YOU.

LET THE CHILDREN PRAISE HIM, THEY ARE THE APPLES OF HIS EYE, AS THEY DANCE WITH ALL THEIR MIGHT AND FLOAT LIKE A BUTTERFLY.

LITTLE JR.

HE IS VIEWING LIFE AS SO UNFAIR, MOMMY NEVER TAUGHT ME, DADDY WAS NOT THERE.

HE NEEDED CORRECTION, HE WANTED LOVE, THE WAY HE KNEW WAS TO FIGHT OR SHOVE.

HIS LIFE WAS A SHELL OF WHAT IT COULD BE, HE SAYS I'LL KILL YOU IF YOU CROSS ME.

HE WAS VIEWING LIFE AS SO UNFAIR, MOMMY NEVER TAUGHT HIM, DADDY WAS NOT THERE.

GOD SAID JR PUT DOWN THE GUN, I WILL BE YOUR FARTHER, YOU CAN BE MY SON.

LOVE WON

SOMETIMES WE FEEL WE HAVE LOST AT LOVE, AS WE LOOK FOR THE SUN,

WHEN WE LOOK AT THE GOOD AND BAD, WE FIND THAT LOVE WON.

GOD GAVE US HIS VERY BEST, WHEN ALL OUR LIVES WERE SUCH A MESS.

THE LOVE NEEDED WAS ALWAYS THERE, HIS PEOPLE WOULD COME FROM EVERYWHERE.

THOSE TIMES WE REACHED OUR LOW POINTS, NOT KNOWING WHAT TO DO,

GOD ALWAYS HAD SOMEONE THERE JUST FOR YOU.

WHEN OTHERS GIVE UP AND WALKED AWAY, HE WILL SEND SOMEONE ALONG,

THEY WILL BE THERE TO LIFT YOUR SPIRIT; GOD WILL GIVE YOU ANOTHER SONG.

SO AT THE TIMES YOU FEEL LET DOWN, REMEMBER JESUS STILL WEARS THE CROWN,

GOD SENT FORTH HIS ONLY SON AND WE ARE STILL HERE TODAY ALL BECAUSE

LOVE WON.

ME, YOU AND ALI BOO

I FELL IN LOVE WITH JUST ONE GLANCE, WITH YOU I NEVER STOOD A CHANCE,

WHO IS THIS PRETTY LITTLE BABY, WILL I STICK AROUND, WELL MAYBE.

I DID NOT KNOW THAT I WOULD STAY, WHILE OTHERS TURNED AND WALKED AWAY.

I DID NOT KNOW THAT SHE WOULD BE, THE ONE GOD USE TO SPEAK TO ME.

THERE WERE TIMES NO ONE WOULD UNDERSTAND, ALI BOO WOULD COME AND HOLD MY HAND.

WITH BOOKS AND PAPER PENCILS AND GLUE, THE LORD ATTACHED ME TO ALI BOO.

WE HUNG IN THERE AND WE WERE TRUE, YES, ME AND YOU AND ALI BOO.

MY FAVORITE PLACE

GOD'S PRESENCE IS ALL AROUND, LOVE PEACE AND JOY ABOUND.

PRAYERS ARE ANSWERED ALL THE TIME, THERE IS NO COST NOT ONE THIN DIME.

SOMETHINGS ARE HARD TO UNDERSTAND, HOW DESPITE MY FALLS HE HOLDS MY HAND.

I KNOW I AM HERE ONLY BY YOUR GRACE, LORD KEEP ME IN MY FAVORITE PLACE.

MY FRIEND – JESUS ARMS

YOU WERE THERE WHEN TIMES WAS ROUGH, WHEN THERE WAS LOVE BUT NOT ENOUGH.

YOU TOOK TIME TO PRAY FOR ME, WHEN THERE WERE TIMES I COULD NOT SEE.

WE WERE FRIENDS IN TIMES OF STORMS, FLYING THROUGH THE STORM IN JESUS ARMS.

MY FRIEND

THAT SPECIAL DAY IS NOT FAR AWAY AND I THINK OF YOU MY FRIEND.

YOU WERE THERE FOR ME, I WAS THERE FOR YOU. WE WERE ALL TOGETHER, YES THE CHILDREN TOO.

WE WENT OUR WAYS AND MADE OUR CHOICE, I STILL LIGHT UP WHEN I HEAR YOUR VOICE.

WE ARE STILL SO MANY MILES AWAY; AS WE LOOK FOR THAT SPECIAL DAY.

THERE ARE MANY TIMES I SEE YOUR FACE, AND WE STILL SHARE THAT SPECIAL PLACE.

LIVE THE LIFE AND PREACH THE WORD, LET THE MESSAGE OF THE CROSS BE HEARD.

WE CAN BOTH LOOK BACK AND REMEMBER WHEN, I WOULD LIKE TO SAY, I MISS YOU SO, MY FRIEND.

MY STORY

BROKEN WOUNDED IN DESPAIR, THE LOVE OF GOD MET ME THERE.

I USE TO HAVE MY DRINK OF CHOICE, NOW TODAY I HEAR HIS VOICE.

I WAS OUT THERE IN THE DANGER ZONE, WHEN JESUS CARE WAS REALLY SHOWN.

THE CLUB WAS CLOSING RIGHT AT TWO, THEY SAID ONE MORE DRINK BUT NOT FOR YOU.

WHEN I THOUGHT LIFE WAS ALL SO SWEET, DEATH WAS OUT THERE IN THE STREET. I WAS SO BLIND I COULD NOT SEE, EVERYTHING WAS JUST FOR ME.

COMPASSION FOR OTHERS I DID NOT KNOW, WHERE THERE IS LOVE IT WILL ALWAYS SHOW.

LORD THE THINGS OF LIFE YOU TOOK ME THROUGH, I GIVE MY LIFE AND THE PRAISE TO YOU.

NO LONGER THERE

WE COME OUT OF DARKNESS INTO YOUR LIGHT, OUR EYES ARE NOW OPEN FOR YOU GAVE US SIGHT.

IN ALL THE THINGS LORD THAT YOU HAVE DONE, THROUGH THE STORMS OF LIFE WE AGAIN SEE THE SUN.

YOUR GRACE AND MERCY IS WHAT BROUGHT US THROUGH, WITH ALL OF OUR HEART LORD WE NOW COME TO YOU.

THE MEMORIES OF OUR PAST WE WILL LEAVE BEHIND, ALTHOUGH THERE WILL BE THE TIMES THEY MAY COME TO MIND.

NEW FRIENDS WE WILL FIND AS WE TRAVEL THE ROAD, LIFE BEING SO MUCH BETTER WITHOUT THE HEAVY LOAD.

THINGS WILL TRY TO STOP US BUT WE MUST LET THEM GO, WE MUST MOVE INTO OUR FUTURE AND NOT LIVE THERE ANYMORE.

NOT BEING FREE

WHILE LOOKING FOR MISCHIEF JUST FOR FUN, YOU WERE YELLING OUT LOUD AND PACKING A GUN.

ALWAYS PEEPING AROUND CORNERS BUT COULD NEVER SEE, YOU WAS LOCKED UP IN YOUR MIND WISHING TO BE FREE,

THE BABIES WERE COMING LEFT AND RIGHT, YOUR CHILD SUPPORT PAYMENTS WERE OUT OF SIGHT.

YOU NEVER KNEW YOUR HISTORY, TRUSTING ONLY IN THE THINGS YOU COULD TOUCH AND SEE.

YOU WERE LACKING IN THE WISDOM OF WHAT IS RIGHT, RUNNING OUT THERE IN THE STREETS DAY AND NIGHT.

YOU WERE RELEASED FROM JAIL SAYING NOW I AM FREE, STILL YELLING ON THE CORNER; WANT TO BE LIKE ME.

SEARCHING FOR WHAT YOU NEEDED BUT COULD NOT SEEM TO FIND, YOU WERE PLAYING THOSE GAMES THAT ARE MOSTLY IN THE MIND.

IT MAKES NO MATTER WHERE YOU COME FROM OR WHAT YOU WANT TO BE,

I KNOW THIS MAN NAME JESUS THAT CAN REALLY SET YOU FREE.

OBSTACLES

OBSTACLES WILL GET IN YOUR WAY, WE MUST KEEP MOVING DAY BY DAY.

WE MUST KEEP CLIMBING TRY NOT TO FALL, YOU MUST BE DETERMINED TO CLIMB THE WALL.

LIFE IS A CHALLENGE AT ITS BEST, WE MUST BE PREPARED TO PASS THE TEST.

GOD IS ALWAYS WITH US SO NEVER DOUBT, WHEN YOU TRUST IN HIM HE WILL BRING YOU OUT.

OBSTACLES WILL COME TRY NOT TO FALL, WE MUST MOVE FORWARD WHILE STANDING TALL.

POVERTY AND PAIN

WILL I BE A MILLIONAIRE OR WILL I EVER LOVE AGAIN, SOME THINGS ARE BORN OUT OF POVERTY AND PAIN.

WE HAVE COME OUT OF ALLEYS AND OFF OF THE STREET, DO WE SHOW THE LOVE OF GOD TO THE PEOPLE WE MEET.

WE MUST KEEP GOING THERE IS NO TIME TO SLOW DOWN NOW WE HAVE TO MAKE IT ON THIS ROCKY ROAD SOMEHOW.

HOLD YOUR HEAD UP HIGH MOVE FORWARD NEVER QUIT, JESUS GAVE HIS LIFE FOR OUR BENEFIT.

I MAY NEVER BE A MILLIONAIRE BUT I WILL CHOOSE TO LOVE AGAIN, GREAT THINGS ARE BORN OUT OF POVERTY AND PAIN.

PUT IT DOWN

PUT DOWN THAT BOTTLE, THROW AWAY THAT CAN, GET RID OF THE PIPE THAT'S IN YOUR HAND.

WE KNOW THAT YOU HAVE LOST YOUR WIFE, STILL YOU MUST GO ON WITH YOUR LIFE.

COME OUT FROM UNDER THE WINE O TREE, THERE IS MUCH MORE THAT YOU CAN BE.

STOP WASTING DAYS JUST GETTING HIGH, THE GOOD TIMES OF LIFE ARE PASSING BY.

THE YEARS ROLL BY AND WE GROW OLD, THE PREACHER STILL FISHES FOR OUR SOUL.

SO PUT DOWN THAT BOTTLE, LET GO THAT CAN, I KNOW YOU CAN BE A BETTER MAN, IF YOU STAND UP AND TAKE YOUR STAND.

RADIANCE

GOD'S RADIANT GLOW NOW WILL SHOW,

AFTER THE STORMS OF LIFE, AFTER THE GUN AND KNIFE.

GOD CHOSE YOU TO BE HIS BEAUTIFUL FLOWER, WHEN IT SEEMED TO BE YOUR DARKEST HOUR.

NOW HIS RADIANT GLOW WILL SHOW, WILL SHOW, LOVE, FAITH AND CONFIDENCE RESTORED,

YOU BLOSSOM AGAIN YOU SWAY IN THE WIND.

YOU ARE NOW A TESTIMONY OF GOD'S LOVE,

YOU NOW SHARE HIS WORD WITH OTHERS, WHILE YOU PREACH AND TEACH THE GOSPEL.

GOD'S VERY RADIANT WOMAN, HIS GLOW WILL NOW SHOW.

SILENCE

WORDS NEVER UTTERED, THOUGH WE FEEL THEM DEEP WITHIN, CLOSENESS NOT DESCRIBED, LIKE THE CLOSENESS OF A FRIEND.

WORDS WE KNOW ARE THERE BUT NEVER COME TO MIND. MATTERS OF THE HEART WE CAN NOT SEEM TO FIND.

WE KNOW THAT IT IS WINTER WHEN SNOW IS EVERYWHERE, A FRIEND THAT SITS IN SILENCE BUT WE KNOW HOW MUCH THEY CARE,

IF I COULD WRITE THE WORDS WHAT WOULD I HAVE TO SAY THE FEELINGS ARE STILL THERE BUT THE WORDS HAVE SLIPPED AWAY.

THERE ARE SO MANY YEARS THAT WE HAVE BEEN APART, I MAY NOT SAY THE WORDS BUT THEY ARE ALWAYS IN MY HEART.

SILENCE, SILENCE, I THINK OF YOU IN SILENCE.

SOMETIMES

SOMETIMES WE LOOK TO OTHERS, WHEN THINGS ARE VERY HARD. WHEN THE MANY THINGS THAT WE ACCEPT, DO NOT BRING US TO GOD.

GOD CALLS US TO THAT SECRET PLACE, AND GIVES US WHAT WE NEED. WHILE THE VARIOUS THINGS THAT WE GO THROUGH, SEEM OH SO ROUGH INDEED.

ONE DAY WE WILL TELL THE STORY, WE WILL GLADLY GIVE GOD THE GLORY.

WHEN THE LIFE WE LIVE IS NO LONGER THE SAME, WE WILL SING PRAISES TO JESUS NAME.

WILL IT BE THE LIFE WE LIVE
WILL IT BE THE SERVICE WE GIVE
WILL IT BE OUR LIGHT THAT SHINE
WILL IT BE OUR PEACE OF MIND

WILL IT BE THE ONES WE HAVE BECOME, THAT WILL MAKE ALL THE DIFFERENCE.

SUCCESS – HOLD JESUS CLOSE

WE GIVE IT ALL WE HAVE WITHOUT THE PAY; WHEN TIMES GET TOUGH FRIENDS WALK AWAY.

THINGS COME AGAINST US AT OUR VERY BEST, ON OUR WAY FORWARD WE MUST PASS THE TEST.

SOME WILL STAY WHILE OTHERS WILL GO, HABITS WE WILL DROP AND NOT PICK UP ANY MORE.

GOD MOVES IN HIS TIME AND GIVES US WHAT WE NEED, HE WILL SURELY SLOW US DOWN IF WE PICK UP TOO MUCH SPEED.

GOOD FRIENDS WE WILL FIND WHEN WE NEED THEM MOST, SO TREAT PEOPLE RIGHT AND HOLD JESUS CLOSE.

SUCCESS – ON THE ROAD

YOU MIGHT WORK ALL DAY, NEVER GET THE RIGHT PAY,

ON THE ROAD TO SUCCESS FRIENDS MAY WALK AWAY.

IT IS PAVED WITH DISAPPOINTMENT, JEALOUSY, AND GREED,

A FEW THINGS WE GO THROUGH TO GET THE THINGS WE NEED.

ALWAYS LIFT YOUR HEAD UP NEVER LET THEM SEE YOU FROWN,

WHILE YOU ARE THERE TAKE THE TIME TO LOOK AROUND.

THE LORD WILL KEEP AND ALWAYS SEE YOU THROUGH,

AND THERE WILL BE TIMES YOU ARE NOT SURE WHAT TO DO.

WALK THIS ROAD WITH STRENGTH, LOOK UP AS YOU STRIDE,

YES, AND BY THE WAY YOU MAY FIND A LOVELY BRIDE.

WALK THE ROAD WELL BE SURE TO PASS THE TEST,

ALTHOUGH IT MIGHT GET ROUGH AND ROCKY, ON THE ROAD TO SUCCESS.

SUGAR PLUM

WE GO THROUGH THINGS NOW AND THEN, SUGAR PLUM SEEMS TO HAVE LOST A FRIEND.

SWEET AND GENTLE IS HER WAY, GOD GETS THE PRAISE FOR HER DAY.

THE SUN SHINES BRIGHTLY FROM ABOVE, SUGAR PLUM HAS A HEART OF LOVE.

WE ARE ALL TOGETHER IN THIS PLACE, AND WE ALL MUST RUN THIS RACE.

JUST TRUST IN JESUS ALL THE WAY, WE ARE LOOKING FOR A GREATER DAY.

THERE ARE MANY THINGS THAT GOD WILL DO. JUST NOT FOR SUGAR PLUM ALSO FOR YOU.

THINGS WILL WORK OUT AFTER A WHILE, SUGAR PLUM HAS BACK HER BEAUTIFUL SMILE.

SUNNY DAYS

PEOPLE SAILING, BABIES CRYING, CHILDREN LAUGHING, MY FRIEND IS DYING.

I SIT TO REFLECT ON THE DAY, NOW I AM SEEING LIFE IN A DIFFERENT WAY

A DAY WE HAVE WITH LOVE TO GIVE, OUR FRIENDS WE MEET AND THE LIFE WE LIVE.

I SEE HER AS SHE GOES DOWN FAST, THOSE VERY GOOD MEMORIES OF THE PAST.

THERE IS THIS SPECIAL TWINKLE IN HER EYE SAYING NOT TO WORRY OR WONDER WHY.

JESUS IS THE ONE THAT IS IN CONTROL, HE IS MY FRIEND AND WATCHES OVER MY SOUL.

SWEETNESS

CONDELISA DOES IT MEANS SOMETHING SWEET, YOU ARE SO BEAUTIFUL, STRONG AND NEAT.

WE CALL YOU SWEETNESS YOU ARE SMART AND SMOOTH. YOU ARE A STRONG BLACK WOMAN ON THE MOVE.

WE SAY YOUR NAME WE SAY IT LOUD, PERFORM YOUR JOB AND MAKE US PROUD.

WE LOVE YOU SWEETNESS WE WISH YOU WELL, WE KNOW THAT ONE DAY HISTORY WILL SURELY TELL,

THE GREAT STORY OF THE LADY WE CALL SWEETNESS.

THANK YOU JESUS

I WAS DOWN ON THE CORNER OUT ON THE STREET, GENTLY USED CLOTHES, NOT DRESSED TOO NEAT.

MY MIND IS NOT GOOD, WILL YOU HELP ME PLEASE, I FEEL A NEED TO REPENT SO I HIT MY KNEES.

THE WEATHER IS SO COLD AS I WALK THROUGH THE DAY, IF MOMMA COULD SEE ME NOW, WHAT WOULD SHE HAVE TO SAY?

JESUS I GIVE YOU THANKS FOR ALWAYS BEING THERE, I GIVE YOU THANKS JESUS FOR SHOWING THAT YOU CARE.

THANK YOU MOST OF ALL FOR SAVING ME, THANK YOU JESUS FOR SETTING MY SPIRIT FREE.

YOU ARE SO GOOD I LOVE YOU SO, THANK YOU FOR SHOWING ME THE WAY TO GO.

THANKFUL

GRANDMA SAID DO GOOD IN SCHOOL, SHE KNEW EDUCATION WAS THE RIGHT TOOL.

THE SCHOOL DAYS WITH TEACHERS WHO LOVED US SO, AND WE RAN OUT OF THE HOUSE WHEN GRANDMA SAID GO.

WE WORKED AFTER SCHOOL TO HAVE OUR OWN MONEY, THOSE FRIENDS THAT COULD MAKE ANY THING FUNNY.

LIFE FOR ME WAS GOOD THOUGH IT MAY HAVE BEEN HARD. AND GRANDMA LOVED US ALL BUT SHE DID NOT SPARE THE ROD.

I HAVE TRAVELED PLACES I NEVER THOUGH I WOULD BE. GOD HAS SHOWED ME THINGS UNBELIEVABLE TO SEE.

THAT SPECIAL THING

BEFORE THE MARRIAGE AND DIAMOND RING,

WHAT WAS THAT SPECIAL THING,

BEFORE THE LOVE WAS REALLY THERE,

WHAT WAS THAT SPECIAL THING,

WHAT WAS IT THAT ATTRACTED YOU, AND STUCK YOU TOGETHER JUST LIKE GLUE.

WHAT WAS THAT SPECIAL THING

WAS IT SOMETHING YOU COULD FEEL, THAT CLOSED THE CASE AND SEALED THE DEAL

WILL IT STAND THE TEST OF TIME, DO YOU HEAR THE BELLS STILL CHIME

WAS IT ON A SPECIAL DAY THAT SHE TURNED AND LOOKED YOUR WAY

WHAT WAS THAT SPECIAL THING

WAS IT THE GLOW THAT WAS IN HER EYE

THE SPECIAL WAY SHE SAID GOODBYE

WAS IT THE WAY SHE CALLED YOUR NAME AND SINCE YOU'VE NEVER BEEN THE SAME.

WHAT WAS THAT SPECIAL THING

THE CHANNELS OF MY MIND

GRANDMA TOLD ME TO DO GOOD IN SCHOOL, SHE SAID EDUCATION WAS THE VERY BEST TOOL.

THERE WERE SCHOOL DAYS AND TEACHERS WHO LOVED US SO,

WE RAN OUT OF THE HOUSE WHEN IT WAS TIME TO GO.

WE WORKED AFTER SCHOOL TO HAVE OUR OWN MONEY,

ALL THOSE CRAZY FRIENDS WHO THOUGHT EVERYTHING WAS FUNNY.

LIFE FOR ME WAS GOOD THOUGH IT MAY HAVE BEEN HARD,

AND THERE IS NO WAY I COULD HAVE MADE IT WITHOUT THE HELP OF GOD.

MANY GOOD PEOPLE HAVE SHAPED MY LIFE, YES, I THANK THE LORD FOR MY WIFE.

MANY OPPORTUNITIES I HAVE TAKEN, MANY THAT WERE MISSED, MANY HELLOS AND GOODBYES I HAVE KISSED.

I AM STILL THANKFUL FOR THE THINGS I HAVE BEEN THROUGH,

NOW I CAN SEE A BETTER ME AND BELIEVE FOR A BETTER YOU.

THE CHILDREN

THE CHILDREN LIKE TO HAVE THEIR FUN, SEE THEM PLAY, LET THEM RUN.

THEY RUN AROUND, THE GIRLS AND BOYS; BUT ALWAYS LOOK OUT FOR THEIR TOYS.

THEY WILL PICK YOU UP WHEN YOU FEEL LET DOWN, THEY HAVE THE SMILES THAT DESTROYS THE FROWN.

WHEN WE FIGHT BATTLES WE CAN NOT WIN, THE CHILDREN SIT BESIDE US AND BECOME OUR FRIEND.

THERE ARE TIMES WE NEED THE CHILDREN, THERE ARE TIMES THEY NEED US TO, IF WE GIVE THEM LOT'S OF LOVE, THEY WILL BE THERE FOR YOU.

SO JUST LET THE CHILDREN PLAY, LET THE CHILDREN RUN, THEY MIGHT MAKE LOTS OF NOISE BUT THEY'RE JUST HAVING FUN.

THE COUNTRY PREACHER

HE PREACHED TO THE SAVED AND TO THE LOST, HIS MESSAGE WAS JESUS AND THE CROSS.

SOMETIMES HIS WORDS WOULD BEGIN TO RING, THE SISTERS WOULD SHOUT AND THE CHOIR COULD SING.

HIS GREATEST DESIRE WAS TO DO GOD'S WILL, WHILE GOD IS WORKING WITH US STILL.

THERE WERE TIMES THE BILLS WERE RUNNING LATE, PASTOR WOULD GIVE HIS LAST IN THE OFFERING PLATE.

HE WAS A GREAT EXAMPLE TO THE FLOCK, HE PAID LITTLE ATTENTION TO THE CLOCK.

HIS WIFE AND KIDS WERE FAITHFUL TOO, THERE WERE MANY THINGS HE HAD TO DO.

THE CHOIR COULD SING LIKE A BEAUTIFUL BIRD, PASTOR STOOD

FLAT FOOTED AND PREACHED THE WORD.

THE DOCTOR

THE YEARS PASS BY AS SHE ATTEND CLASSES,

SHE REST HER EYES AND TAKES OFF HER GLASSES.

SHE RISES UP EARLY AND STAYS UP LATE,

SHE RUNS TO THE BUS STOP AND STILL HAS TO WAIT.

ALWAYS TRYING TO SUCCEED WITH ALL HER HEART,

THIS VERY BRIGHT YOUNG LADY THAT FITS THE PART.

IT HAS TAKEN HER YEARS BUT NOW YOU SEE,

SHE IS ONLY ONE YEAR FROM HER DOCTORATE DEGREE.

THE EFFECTS OF ABUSE

THERE ARE THINGS IN LIFE WE ALL GO THROUGH,

WHAT MAKES YOU SAY; BUT NOT FOR YOU.

I HEAR YOUR VOICE, I KNOW YOUR PAIN, BUT I WAS IN THE OTHER LANE.

I PRAYED A TOTAL OF SEVEN YEARS, CRIED OUT AT MIDNIGHT IN MY TEARS.

MY HOPES AND DREAMS WERE ALL SO HIGH, YOU CAME TO TALK AND SAID GOODBYE.

THOSE VOWS WE TOOK, WHAT DO THEY MEAN, WHEN WE HOLD THINGS THAT ARE NOT SEEN.

WAS IT TOO MUCH HEARTACHE; TOO MUCH PAIN, BUT I WAS IN THE OTHER LANE.

I VOWED TO BE LOVING AND TO BE TRUE, AND STILL YOU SAID; BUT NOT FOR YOU.

I KNOW IT MAY NOT HAVE BEEN GOD'S PLAN, SO I WILL WALK ON AS A GODLY MAN.

THOSE OTHER THINGS I DID NOT DO, AND I WILL ALWAYS PRAY FOR YOU.

WAS IT ALL THOSE THINGS THEY PUT YOU TROUGH,

WHY DO YOU SAY; BUT NOT FOR YOU.

THE FLAWS

WE SEE THE FLAWS IN PEOPLES LIVES, AND WE TEND TO WALK AWAY.

WE TURN OUR HEADS AND SHUT OUR MOUTHS, WHAT WILL THE OTHERS SAY.

WHERE IS THE LOVE THAT WE ONCE HAD, TO HELP EACH OTHER THROUGH

WE SEE THE FLAWS IN OTHERS LIVES, BUT NOT THE FLAWS FOR YOU.

THEY MAY HAVE WALKED THE RIGHTEOUS PATH BUT SLIPPED JUST FOR A WHILE,

WILL WE BE WILLING TO LEND A HAND, ENCOURAGED BY A SMILE.

WE ALL HAVE FLAWS BUT BY GOD'S GRACE, WE WILL MAKE IT IN THE END.

WE SEE THE FLAWS, WE SEE THE FLAWS, IN THIS OLD WORLD OF SIN.

THE LADY

YOU APPEARED AT THE TIME I NEED A FRIEND, HARDLY KNOWING ME YOU STEPPED RIGHT IN.

IT WAS NOT FOR MONEY NOR WAS IT FOR FAME, IF THAT HAD BEEN THE CASE YOU WOULD NOT HAVE KNOWN MY NAME.

GOD SENDS GOOD FRIENDS AND WE FIND THEM TO BE FEW, WHAT WOULD HAVE HAPPENED HAD I NOT MET YOU?

THERE WERE TIMES I WAS IN DOUBT, OTHER TIMES IN FEAR, WHENEVER I NEEDED A FRIEND I WISH YOU COULD BE THERE.

GOD IN HIS MERCY SENT YOU WHEN TIMES WAS HARD, YOU ARE STILL HERE AFTER ALL THESE YEARS AND I GIVE THANKS TO GOD.

THE LIONESS

YOUNG ALERT AND STRONG, THINGS GET QUIET AS SHE MOVES ALONG.

HER STATURE IS BEYOND COMPARE,

CAN YOU SEE THE YOUNG LIONESS STANDING THERE

SHE IS STANDING WITH NO TIME TO WASTE, BOLDLY RIGHT BEFORE YOUR FACE.

DID SOMETHING MOVE, WHAT WAS THAT SOUND,

ONE LEAP AND SHE CAN PUT YOU DOWN.

THE LITTLE CHILD

WE LOOKED AND WE BEGIN TO SMILE, THEY COULD NOT KEEP HER FROM THE CENTER AISLE.

WE GAVE GOD PRAISE AS SHE CLAPPED HER HANDS, THE DAY IS GONE BUT THE MEMORY STILL STANDS.

JESUS YOU ARE SO MEEK AND MILD, THAT ALSO YOU WOULD USE THIS CHILD.

THE PREACHER GAVE THE MESSAGE STANDING ON THE STAGE, AND THE TWO YEAR OLD GIRL GAVE HER MOST AWESOME PRAISE.

THE MASTER

THE MASTER WALKS ALONG THE SEA,
HE IS LOVING HIS CHILDREN YOU
AND ME.

WILL WE LOVE HIM MOST OF ALL,
WILL WE ANSWER WHEN WE HEAR
HIM CALL

CAN WE LEAN ON HIM TO BE STRONG
CAN WE TRUST IN HIM AS WE MOVE
ALONG

WE MUST GIVE GLORY TO HIS NAME,
IN HIM WE WILL NEVER BE THE
SAME.

HE IS OUR SAVIOR MASTER, FRIEND,
IF HE SHOULD KNOCK WILL YOU LET
HIM

IN GOD BRINGS THE BRIGHTNESS TO
OUR DAYS, GIVE GOD A HA LA LU AH
PRAISE.

THE NICKEL

IT HAPPENED MANY YEARS AGO WHEN TIMES WERE ROUGH,

I FOUND MYSELF COLLECTING CHANGE BUT NOT ENOUGH.

I LOOKED AROUND AND SHE WAS THERE, SHE STOPPED AND SET BY ME,

I KNEW SHE HAD A LOVING HEART AND LOVE BEYOND DEGREE.

WE SAT AND WE TALKED AWHILE, THERE WERE THINGS SHE HAD TO SAY,

SHE BLESSED ME WITH A NICKEL AND THEN SHE WALKED AWAY.

THE OTHER SIDE OF LOVE

I SEE JESUS AS HE HANGED UPON THE TREE, HE SUFFERED AND DIED TO REDEEM YOU AND ME.

HE WAS WIPED, SPIT UPON AND PIERCED IN HIS SIDE, HE SAID FATHER FORGIVES THEM, HE GAVE UP THE GHOST AND HE DIED.

WHEN I VIEW THE CROSS I FEEL A GENTLE SHOVE, I SEE JESUS HANGING THERE; I SEE THE OTHER SIDE OF LOVE.

A LOVE SO DEEP THE MIND CANNOT COMPREHEND, THAT EVERLASTING LOVE THAT DELIVERS US FROM SIN.

THE LOVE OF THE FATHER SO GREAT FOR YOU AND ME, HE SENT HIS ONLY SON TO DIE ON THE TREE.

IT WAS ALL A PART OF GOD'S MASTER PLAN, I SEE JESUS ON THE TREE WITH NAILS IN HIS HAND.

ONLY HIS BLOOD THAT WAS SHED COULD TRULY SET US FREE, ON THE OTHER SIDE OF LOVE JESUS DIED FOR YOU AND ME.

THE PARK

IN THE COOL SHADE OF THE TREES, SITTING IN THE EVENING BREEZE.

ALL THOSE HAPPY DAYS WE WERE SO AMAZED, NOW OUR LIVES HAVE CHANGED IN SO MANY WAYS.

PLAYING BASKET BALL TILL DARK, GAMES AND HORSE RIDES IN THE PARK.

WE LIVE OUR LIVES WE PAY THE PRICE, WHEN WE GET STRESSED THE PARK SEEMS NICE.

SOME LOST THEIR MATES SAID IT WAS FINE, THANK YOU GOD WE DID NOT LOSE OUR MIND.

IF THERE COMES A TIME THAT YOU NEED ME, THEN THE PARK IS LIKELY WHERE I WILL BE.

ALL THOSE HAPPY DAYS WE WERE SO AMAZED, NOW OUR LIVES HAVE CHANGED IN SO MANY WAYS.

THE QUEEN

SHE COMMANDS ATTENTION AND RESPECT, THE LIFE SHE LIVES HAS THAT EFFECT.

A LOVELY LADY HUMBLE AND KIND, SHE IS THE QUEEN WITH GOD ON HER MIND.

HERE SHE COMES DOWN THE HALL WITH THAT BEAUTIFUL SMILE, WHEN YOU LOOKED SOMEPLACE ELSE, SHE WAS THERE ALL THE WHILE.

SHE KNEW YOUR PAIN WHEN YOU KNEW NOT WHAT TO DO, THE QUEEN CAME YOUR WAY AND YOU MADE IT THROUGH.

A VERY REAL LADY IS SO HARD TO FIND, SHE IS THE QUEEN WITH GOD ON HER MIND.

THE RAIN 2

I WAS RUNNING NINETY MILES AN HOUR, WITH A HEART FULL OF PAIN... WHEN I HEARD A SWEET VOICE SAY, I LIKE TO WALK IN THE RAIN.

THE RAIN WAS GENTLY FALLING DOWN, I ONLY TOOK THE TIME TO LOOK AROUND.

WHEN IN MY PAIN I DID NOT SEE, SHE WAS ONLY THERE TO COMFORT ME.

GOD WAS SAYING PLEASE BE STILL, SLOW DOWN SO YOU CAN DO MY WILL.

I WAS CAUGHT UP IN MY POSITION, THOUGH GOD GIVES US INTUITION.

WE CAN LOSE SOME VERY PRECIOUS THINGS, IN THE MIST OF OUR PAIN, WHAT IF I HAD WALKED IN THE RAIN...

THE SPARKLE

HOW MUCH HE LOVES US WE WILL ALWAYS KNOW, LIFE MOVES SWIFTLY AND AWAY WE GO.

WHENEVER WE LIFT HIS NAME ON HIGH, WE ARE THE SPARKLE IN JESUS EYE.

WE WALK AWAY COME BACK AGAIN, WE GIVE OUR LAST TO HELP A FRIEND.

HIS EYES WATCHES OVER YOU AND I, JESUS KNOWS THE ANSWER TO THE QUESTION WHY.

HE SEE US DOING OUR STORMS AND RAIN, HE SEES OUR HURT, HE FEELS THE PAIN.

ALTHOUGH TIMES WILL COME THAT WE NEED TO CRY, WE ARE STILL THAT SPARKLE IN JESUS EYE.

THE TEST OF LOVE

FORGIVENESS IS THE TEST OF LOVE, WHAT I WOULD CHOOSE TO SAY,

GOD'S TENDER MERCIES FROM ABOVE, HIS IS THE ONLY WAY.

ALONG THE WAY WE STRAY SOMETIMES, WE FIND THAT ALL'S NOT LOSS,

JESUS PAID THE PRICE FOR US, WHEN HE DIED ON THE CROSS.

WILL WE CHOOSE TO FORGIVE,

JUST FOR JESUS WILL WE LIVE.

I KNOW OF NO BETTER WAY, TO LIVE IN HAPPINESS DAY BY DAY.

GOD SENDS THE RAVEN AND THE DOVE.

FORGIVENESS IS THE TEST OF LOVE.

THE VIEW

THE BIRDS ASCENDING IN THE CONNECTICUT SKY, THERE ARE PEOPLE AT LUNCH TIME WALKING BRISTLY BY.

THE WHITE CLOUDS HANG OVER THE BEAUTIFUL GREEN HILL, SUCH A LOVELY VIEW THAT GIVES THE TRILLS.

THE YOUNG MEN WITH SKATEBOARDS PASSING TIME. IN THE DISTANCE I HEAR THE CHURCH BELL CHIME.

CARS SLOWLY WINDING AROUND THE CURVE, AS THE BREEZE IS GENTLY BLOWING, IT IS LUNCH TIME AT THE PARK, EVERY ONE IS GOING.

A VERY BEAUTIFUL DAY, WITH A WONDERFUL VIEW, THIS IS THE KIND OF DAY THAT WILL GET US THROUGH.

LORD THANK YOU FOR THE BIRTHDAY PRESENT YOU SENT MY

WAY, YOU ARE SO GOOD AND YOU ARE THERE EVERYDAY.

THERE WERE TIMES I FOCUSED ON WHAT I WAS GOING THROUGH, TODAY I FIND MYSELF LIVING FOR YOU.

IT IS A BEAUTIFUL DAY, WITH A WONDERFUL VIEW, AND IT IS LUNCH TIME AT THE PARK.

VIOLENCE

LET US TALK AND WORK IT OUT, THERE NEVER HAS TO BE A BOUT.

WE SHOULD LISTEN AND CHOOSE ANOTHER WAY, THERE IS TOO MUCH VIOLENCE IN THE WORLD TODAY.

VIOLENCE, THIS WORLD IS OUT OF SHAPE, VIOLENCE, VIOLENCE, NO ESCAPE.

THE STORM IS RAGING DOWN COMES THE RAIN, WE DO THINGS FOR OUR OWN SELFISH GAIN.

WE REJECT GOD AND CROOKEDNESS SITS IN, VIOLENCE IN A WORLD THAT IS FULL OF SIN

THIS VERY WELL COULD BE OUR LAST DAY, WHILE MANY THINK VIOLENCE IS STILL THE WAY.

THERE WILL COME A DAY WHEN VIOLENCE WILL CEASE, AND WE WILL LOOK TO JESUS FOR HE IS OUR PEACE.

WANDA

BEAUTIFUL VISIONS OF YOU SINCE YOU HAVE GONE AWAY, YOU WERE BEAUTIFUL, SO BEAUTIFUL.

I SEE YOU WITH THE PRETTY SMILE, YOUR BIG BROWN EYES AND I THINK AWHILE.

WE WENT THROUGH THE FIRE AND WE WON, THE THINGS OF THIS LIFE MATTER NONE.

GOD HEARD OUR PLEA, AND ANSWERED OUR PRAYS, GOD SHOWED US HIS LOVE AND WE KNOW HE CARES.

HE WANTED US TO KNOW WHAT HE HAS DONE, IN THE FULLNESS OF TIME, HE SENT FORTH HIS SON.

I MUST TAKE THIS JOURNEY AND AS I GO ON, THE HOLY SPIRIT WILL GUIDE ME, FOR I WILL NOT BE ALONE.

THE BATTLE HAS BEEN FOUGHT AND THE VICTORY WON, GOD WANTED US TO SEE IT IS ALREADY DONE.

WE WHO WORE

WE FIGHT UNTIL THE VICTORY IS WON, WE WHO WORE THE BIG RED ONE.

THEY DROPPED US DOWN IN A HORNETS NEST, WE HAVE BEEN TRAINED TO FIGHT OUR BEST.

GUNSHIPS FIGHTING FROM THE SKY, NEVER KNOWING IF YOU WILL LIVE OR DIE.

WE LOOK FOR RAIN, SWEAT IN THE SUN, WE WHO WORE THE BIG RED ONE.

OUR BUDDIES DYING IN OUR FACE, HOW DID I GET IN THIS PLACE?

WE STILL STOOD TALL AND WE WERE TRUE, WE DID THE THINGS WE HAD TO DO.

WE FIGHT UNTIL THE VICTORY IS WON, WE WHO WORE THE BIG RED ONE.

WHEN LEAST EXPECTED

MY EYES WERE OPENED, NOW I CAN SEE, YOUR LOVE IS EVERYTHING TO ME.

MY HEART HAS BEEN CHANGED BEYOND COMPARE, LORD ON MY KNEES I MET YOU THERE.

WISDOM AND KNOWLEDGE WERE INCREASED, YOU BROKE THE CHAINS AND BROUGHT RELEASE.

YOU ARE AWESOME GOD IN SO MANY WAYS, THAT IS WHY I GIVE THIS SPECIAL PRAISE.

WHEN I THOUGHT I HAD MY MASTER PLAN, GOD YOU MADE ME A HUMBLE MAN.

YET DURING ALL THE STRESS AND STRIFE, FORGIVENESS BECAME A WAY OF LIFE.

WE HAD GREAT TIMES IN OUR ROMANCE, THEN YOU GAVE ME A HOLY DANCE,

I SAY JESUS, JESUS, AND JESUS. LIFE FOR ME CAN NOT BE THE SAME, ALL THINGS COME IN JESUS NAME.

YOU WERE THERE

GOD HAD YOU THERE AT THE TIMES THAT I WAS GOING THROUGH, THE TIMES YOU SHOWED CONCERN FOR ME, SAID I WILL BE THERE FOR YOU.

WITH A BEAUTIFUL SMILE AND GREAT BIG HUGS YOU CAME ACROSS THE SEA, WHILE I WAS SAILING THROUGH THE STORM GOD HAD YOU THERE FOR ME.

WITH LOVE AND ENCOURAGEMENT YOU KEPT MY SPIRIT HIGH, I SAW YOU DANCE AND GIVE HIM PRAISE BUT I DID NOT SEE YOU CRY.

WITH A SMILING FACE AND BIG BRIGHT EYES YOU MET ME AT THE DOOR, YOU ALWAYS TOOK THAT EXTRA STEP AS YOU USHERED ON THE FLOOR.

THESE WORDS I WRITE ARE JUST A FEW TO EXPRESS MY THANKS, GOD HAD YOU THERE WOMEN OF GOD,

AND THAT IS MORE THAN MONEY IN THE BANKS.

About the Author

Pastor Billy Carr Sr. volunteers in his community as a community activist and street pastor under Second Chance Church in New Britain. He tries to carry the message everywhere he goes, to everyone in need, and those who care to accept what he has to offer. Pastor Carr is also a veteran of the United States Army who served in Vietnam and is going to be 73 years young.

May God Bless you and may his light shine upon you. Amen!

www.ingramcontent.com/pod-product-compliance
Lightning Source LLC
Chambersburg PA
CBHW061956070426
42450CB00011BA/3050